# LEAVES

199 Photographs by

## Andreas Feininger

Dover Publications, Inc.
New York

Cover: Beech leaves unfolding in the spring.

FRONTISPIECE: A mulberry leaf in fall. The design formed by the retreating chlorophyll mirrors the design of a tree, the lateral veins corresponding to the branches, the center vein and stalk to the trunk. There is nothing mysterious about this similarity since the structure of a leaf repeats, on a miniature scale, the basic design of a tree.

**Visual Studies Workshop**
**Research Center**
**Rochester, N.Y.**
Oct 14, 1985
Gift of the publisher

Published in Canada by General Publishing Company, Ltd., 30 Lesmill Road, Don Mills, Toronto, Ontario.
Published in the United Kingdom by Constable and Company, Ltd., 10 Orange Street, London WC2H 7EG.

*Leaves: 199 Photographs by Andreas Feininger* is a new work, first published by Dover Publications, Inc., in 1984. Chapter I is adapted from "Feininger's Guide to Identifying Trees," as published in *Horticulture*, June 1977.

Manufactured in the United States of America
Dover Publications, Inc., 31 East 2nd Street, Mineola, N.Y. 11501

**Library of Congress Cataloging in Publication Data**

Feininger, Andreas, 1906–
  Leaves : 199 photographs.

  Includes index.
  1. Leaves—Pictorial works.   I. Title.
QK649.F35   1984      582.16'0497      83-20532
ISBN 0-486-24650-7

# Contents

# Foreword

Leaves—together with the phytoplankton of the sea—are the most important structures in nature. They are the factories that produce not only the food, but also the oxygen, without which life on earth could not exist.

The process by which this miracle is achieved is photosynthesis. The energy that powers it is light. What happens is this: Within the structure of the leaf, under the influence of light, with chlorophyll serving as the catalyst in a highly complex reaction still not fully understood, six molecules of carbon dioxide taken from the air combine with six molecules of water taken from the ground to yield one molecule of sugar—glucose—and six molecules of oxygen. It is this single molecule of sugar, multiplied by the astronomical number of such molecules synthesized each second, that is the basis of all life.

No one can grasp the true magnitude of this operation in quantitative terms, although it can be expressed in numbers. Who can visualize a billion tons? Yet it is in such terms we must think when we want to understand the extent of photosynthesis. This is what science tells us: Year in, year out, the plants of the world produce some 250 billion tons of sugar (for comparison, man's annual sugar harvest is less than 40 million tons). Sugar is chemical energy in fixed form, and the annual amount of energy produced in this way by plants, if released by burning, would come to some three quintillion kilocalories (a 3 followed by 18 zeros). This is about 100 times the amount of energy we could produce if we burned all the coal mined during one year in the entire world.

While manufacturing glucose, leaves release oxygen. This liberated oxygen is just as vital to the continuance of life as the sugar produced by plants. For, although oxygen is one of the most abundant elements on earth, most of it is chemically fixed in the form of water or as an oxide. In addition, large amounts of oxygen are constantly withdrawn from the atmosphere by the respiration of living things; the burning of coal, oil, wood, garbage and other organic compounds; and by natural oxidation processes such as the rusting of iron and the weathering of rocks. And, in the course of time, were it not for the activity of plants, these factors would combine to extract all oxygen from the air. However, although plants use up oxygen in respiration, this amount is smaller than that released by the dissociation of water in photosynthesis. Consequently, more oxygen is released into the air than is withdrawn from it. As a matter of fact, most scientists believe that the protoatmosphere of the primeval earth contained virtually no oxygen and that the present high content of close to 21 percent by volume is largely the result of plant activity. Should this process ever stop—perhaps through destruction of vast areas of forest by man—life on earth would come to an end.

So we can truly say that without leaves, there would be no grain, rice, corn or potatoes; no grass, flowers or trees. As a matter of fact, there would be no plants. And without plants there would, of course, be no plant-eating animals—no cows, horses or sheep, chickens or ducks, rabbits or mice, antelopes or elephants. And without plant-eating animals, flesh-eating animals could not exist—no dogs or cats, lions or wolves, eagles or owls and, of course, no people. Without the activities of leaves, there would be no organic compounds of any kind whatsoever and, except for a few autotrophic bacteria, the world would be as lifeless as the moon.

# A Guide to the Identification of 50 Deciduous Northeastern Trees on the Basis of Leaf Design

Leaves grow in an almost unlimited number of different forms, each plant or tree having developed its own characteristic design in accordance with its needs, modified by, and adapted to, the particular aspects of its environment. As a result, a plant or tree can often be identified by its leaves alone.

However, while this is true in principle, in practice certain difficulties may arise. Although the leaves belonging to a specific tree always adhere to the design characteristic of its species, variations within this design can be surprisingly great. Most people believe that all they have to do to identify a tree is to pick a leaf and compare it with photographs or drawings in a tree-identification book. Although basically sound, this approach can succeed only if the investigator also considers the following:

Leaves often vary within the same species, sometimes to an astonishingly high degree.

If the leaves vary significantly in size or form, pick a representative sample of three, five or more in different shapes.

The leaves on the lower branches of a tree often differ significantly from, and usually are larger than, those closer to the top.

The leaves of saplings and vigorous shoots are often considerably larger than those of mature trees and may even differ in shape.

Try to develop a "feeling" for the design of the leaves of a group of related trees. This will enable you to identify at sight a particular tree as belonging to, say, the dogwoods (although it may be a Japanese import which you may never have seen before), or the maples, the ashes, the black oaks. This is simply a matter of experience, of having examined the leaves of many different trees.

Look for confirmation. Consider, for example, the mode of leaf attachment to the twig, the bark, the flowers and fruit (if present) or other characteristics of the tree such as sap oozing from a broken leaf stalk, the degree of stickiness of a bud, a specific odor of the crushed leaf and so on—clues to identification that will be given later in this guide.

Tree identification on the basis of leaf design is a process of elimination involving four main considerations; by evaluating the design of the respective leaf in regard to four basic characteristics, the investigator can eliminate at a glance whole groups of trees to which his leaf cannot possibly belong because of fundamental differences in design. The four leaf characteristics that must be considered are: leaf design in regard to venation (p. 9); mode of leaf attachment to the twig (p. 10); leaf design in regard to leaf grouping (p. 11); leaf design in regard to margin formation (pp. 12–13). Thus, by ruling out every characteristic that does not fit the design of your leaf, you finally arrive at a group of trees to which your tree must belong. And if still in doubt because the leaves of two or more trees are very similar, information given under the subhead "Confirmation" should eliminate any lingering doubt and enable you to make a positive identification.

# Leaf Design in Regard to Venation

Examine the venation of the leaf—the pattern of the veins that conduct food and water and also serve to stiffen the blade. In respect to venation, a leaf may belong to one of the following groups.

**Parallel Venation.** The chief veins run parallel or nearly so. Typical representatives: ginkgo (RIGHT), the palms.

**Net Venation.** The veins form a netlike pattern. This pattern can take two forms:

**Pinnately Veined Leaves.** A single main vein runs the entire length of the leaf from stalk to tip, with secondary veins branching off laterally like the barbs of a feather. Typical representatives: the oaks, birches, poplars (RIGHT), aspens and elms (FAR RIGHT).

**Palmately Veined Leaves.** Several main veins (three, five or seven) diverge from the juncture of leaf stalk and blade like the fingers of an outspread hand, each running to the tip of a lobe. Typical representatives: sycamore, the maples (RIGHT, the Norway maple), three-lobed sassafras and mulberries (FAR RIGHT, the white mulberry).

# Mode of Leaf Attachment to the Twig

An examination of the order of attachment of the leaves to the twig can speed up the process of identification considerably by instantly eliminating from consideration entire groups of trees. If the leaves grow, say, opposite one another in pairs, the tree in question cannot possibly be one of the oaks, poplars, willows, birches or elms; nor can it be a beech, locust, linden, catalpa, cherry, sassafras, mulberry and so on—all trees whose leaves are arranged in a different order on the branch. In this respect, distinguish between three orders of arrangement.

**Opposite Leaves.** The leaves grow from the twig symmetrically in pairs with one leaf exactly opposite the other. This is a relatively rare form of leaf arrangement, and the few native trees belonging to this group can easily be remembered by memorizing the mnemonic phrase "madcap horse" in which "m" stands for "maple," "a" for "ash," "d" for "dogwood" (flowering), "cap" for the "Caprifoliaceae" to which viburnum belongs and "horse" for "horse chestnut" (and its cousin, buckeye).

**Alternate Leaves.** The leaves grow on the twig asymmetrically instead of opposite, alternating right and left, often in an ascending spiral. This is the most common form of leaf arrangement, represented, among others, by the oaks, birches, willows and elms (ABOVE, the slippery elm).

**Whorled Leaves.** The leaves grow around the twig in clusters of three. This is the least common type of leaf arrangement. A typical representative is catalpa (ABOVE).

# Leaf Design in Regard to Leaf Grouping

Determine to which of the four forms shown on this page a leaf belongs, whether it is *simple* or *compound,* and if compound, whether it is *palmately, pinnately* or *twice pinnately* compound.

**Simple leaf**

A **simple leaf** consists of two and sometimes three parts: (1) an undivided *blade,* the margin of which may be either smooth ("*entire*"), *crenate* (with rounded "teeth"), *serrate* (with pointed "teeth"), *wavy* (undulating) or *lobed* (deeply indented); (2) a stalk (the *petiole*), which in some leaves is absent (such leaves are said to be *sessile*); (3) leaflike, usually small, structures at the base of the stalk called *stipules* (see the black-willow leaf, p. 16). ABOVE: Poplar.

A **compound leaf** consists of three or more blades called *leaflets* attached to a common stalk. To find out whether a cluster of foliage is an aggregate of simple leaves or a single compound leaf, start at what seems to be the tip of the leaf and continue toward the trunk until you arrive at a woody branch or a bud (in late spring, however, these winter buds are absent; in some trees the buds are submerged in the bark). Break off everything to this point, and you hold in your hand the complete leaf. Depending on the way in which the leaflets are arranged, distinguish between three types of compound leaf.

**Palmately Compound.** All the leaflets come together at the tip of the stalk, fanning like the fingers of an outspread hand. Typical representatives: horse chestnut (ABOVE), buckeye, cut-leaf maple.

**Compound leaves.**

**Pinnately compound.** The leaflets are attached on either side of a central stalk like the barbs of a feather (with one leaflet usually at the tip). Typical representatives: black locust (ABOVE), the sumacs, the ashes.

**Twice pinnately compound.** The leaf structure consists of a central stalk with a row of pinnately compound leaves attached to either side. Typical representatives: honey locust (ABOVE), Hercules'-club, Kentucky coffee tree.

# Leaf Design in Regard to Margin Formation

Examine the leaf margin. It can provide important clues to the identity of a tree. In this respect, distinguish between six types.

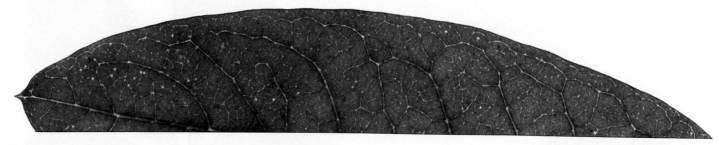

**Entire.** The leaf edge is smooth, has no teeth of any kind and is neither wavy nor lobed. Typical representatives: catalpa, dogwood, the un-lobed leaves of sassafras.

**Wavy.** The leaf edge is smooth but undulating. A typical representative is the chestnut oak.

**Crenate.** The leaf edge bears small, *rounded* teeth. Typical representatives: cottonwood, aspen, white mulberry.

**Serrate.** The leaf margin bears *pointed* teeth like the edge of a saw. Typical representatives: black cherry, linden, American chestnut.

**Twice serrate.** The leaf edge is marked by large teeth which in turn bear smaller teeth. Typical representatives: gray birch, slippery elm, American elm.

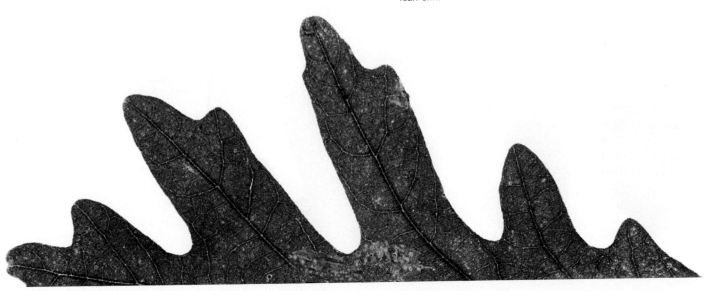

**Lobed.** The spaces between the teeth or waves extend one-third of the way or more toward the center of the leaf. Typical representatives: the maples, many oaks, three-lobed sassafras and mulberry, tulip tree.

**Flowering Dogwood**
*Cornus florida* L.

**Pagoda Dogwood**
*Cornus alternifolia* Lf.

The 3- to 4-inch-long leaves of these two species of dogwood are virtually indistinguishable from one another, especially since both vary from fairly narrow to rather wide. But because of their peculiar kind of venation (the secondary veins run in wide curves to the margins, a type of venation called *arcuate*), both are easily recognizable as dogwoods.

CONFIRMATION: If leaves are opposite, it is flowering dogwood; if leaves are alternate, it is pagoda dogwood. In spring, flowering dogwood carries large white "flowers" (what looks like petals actually are *bracts* that encircle the tiny greenish flowers). The small, cream-colored flowers of pagoda dogwood are rather inconspicuous.

**Catalpa**
*Catalpa bignonioides* Walt.
Leaves large and heart-shaped, 6 to 10 inches long, 4 to 7 inches wide, with prominent midrib and primary veins.
CONFIRMATION: Leaves grow in whorls of three, rarely opposite. In late summer, fall and winter, the tree carries conspicuous 6-to-18-inch-long beans. If the leaves are opposite and the tree has 1-to-1½-inch-long fruit pods instead of beans, it is **paulownia** (*Paulownia tomentosa* [Thunb.] Steud.), an import from China or Japan.

**Sassafras**
*Sassafras albidum* (Nutt.) Nees
Leaves alternate, 2 to 4 inches long.
CONFIRMATION: The same tree carries three distinctly different types of leaves: simple (unlobed), two-lobed (mitten-shaped) and three-lobed.

# Leaf Simple, Margin Wavy

**Chestnut Oak**
*Quercus prinus* L.
Leaves alternate, 3 to 6 inches long, 1½ to 3 inches wide.
CONFIRMATION: Since this is an oak, it bears acorns; the nut is enclosed about *one-third* of its length by a *thin-walled* cup.

# Leaf Simple, Margin Crenate (Rounded Teeth)

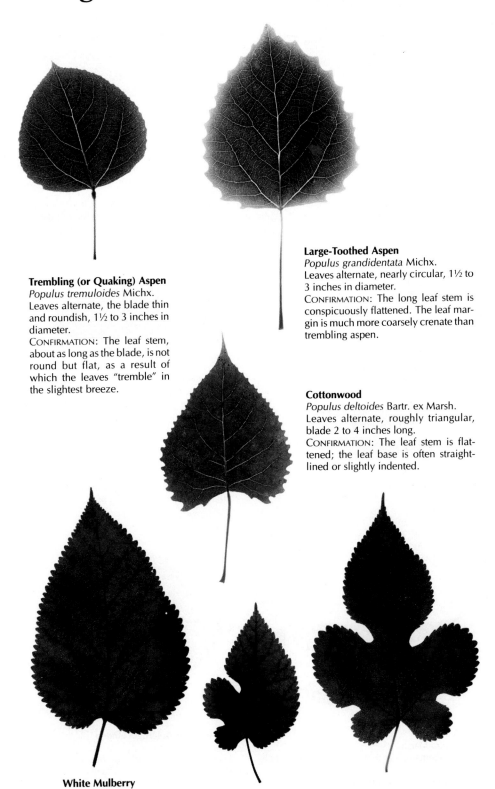

**Trembling (or Quaking) Aspen**
*Populus tremuloides* Michx.
Leaves alternate, the blade thin and roundish, 1½ to 3 inches in diameter.
CONFIRMATION: The leaf stem, about as long as the blade, is not round but flat, as a result of which the leaves "tremble" in the slightest breeze.

**Large-Toothed Aspen**
*Populus grandidentata* Michx.
Leaves alternate, nearly circular, 1½ to 3 inches in diameter.
CONFIRMATION: The long leaf stem is conspicuously flattened. The leaf margin is much more coarsely crenate than trembling aspen.

**Cottonwood**
*Populus deltoides* Bartr. ex Marsh.
Leaves alternate, roughly triangular, blade 2 to 4 inches long.
CONFIRMATION: The leaf stem is flattened; the leaf base is often straight-lined or slightly indented.

**White Mulberry**
*Morus alba* L.
Leaves alternate, 2 to 5 inches long, shiny above. If the top surface is rough and sandpapery, it is red mulberry (*Morus rubra* L.), the leaves of which are larger as a rule. When broken, the leaf stems of both mulberries exude a white sap.

15

# Leaf Simple, Margin Serrate (Pointed Teeth)

### Sweet (or Black) Birch
*Betula lenta* L.

Leaves 2 to 5 inches long, 1½ to 3 inches wide, smooth above, sometimes inconspicuously twice serrate.

CONFIRMATION: Sweet-birch leaves are virtually indistinguishable from hop-hornbeam leaves (p. 17), especially when twice serrate, but the bark of the two trees is very different. The bark of young sweet birches is dark brown, smooth and glossy and patterned with short, white, horizontal "dashes" (*lenticles*); the bark of old sweet birches is scaly and plated. In contrast, the bark of hop hornbeam has a shredded appearance with narrow strips of gray bark covering the trunk like a shaggy fur. Sweet-birch twigs and buds, when chewed, have a strong flavor of wintergreen oil.

### American Beech
*Fagus grandifolia* J. F. Ehrh.

Leaves alternate, 2½ to 5 inches long, 1 to 3½ inches wide, thin with a dry, paperlike feeling, the secondary veins conspicuously parallel, each vein ending in a tooth.

CONFIRMATION: The bark is silvery, thin and smooth, wrinkled in places instead of ridged and cracked as in most other trees, the trunk of old trees looking as if made of cast aluminum.

### American Chestnut
*Castanea dentata* (Marsh.) Borkh.

Leaves alternate, 6 to 8 inches long, 1½ to 2½ inches wide, smooth above and below, sharply serrate with each secondary vein ending in a hair-like point.

CONFIRMATION: Not required. No other tree native to the region has similar leaves. Since chestnut blight killed all the mature trees, American chestnut occurs only in the form of a shrub.

### Black Cherry
*Prunus serotina* J. F. Ehrh.

Leaves alternate, 2 to 6 inches long, 1 to 1½ inches wide, dark and shiny above, lighter below, usually hairy along the midrib near the base.

CONFIRMATION: The bark of young trees is smooth and reddish-brown to nearly black, with long, horizontal, lighter-colored lines (*lenticles*); in older trees, it is scaly and platelike, similar to the bark of sweet birch. Twigs, when chewed, have a characteristic bitter-almond taste.

### Weeping Willow
*Salix babylonica* L.

Leaves alternate, 2 to 5 inches long, dark green above, grayish green below.

CONFIRMATION: The unique character of the tree is marked by its arching branches and long, slim dangling twigs cascading like a waterfall of green leaves.

### Black Willow
*Salix nigra* Marsh.

Leaves alternate, 3 to 5 inches long, ⅜ to ¾ inch wide.

CONFIRMATION: There are *stipules*—small, sickle-shaped, leaflike structures—at the base of the leaf. Conspicuously yellow, long and slender twigs erupt in large numbers from knots in the deeply ridged trunk.

### Basswood or American Linden
*Tilia americana* L.

Leaves alternate, more or less circular heart-shaped, 4 to 6 inches in diameter, often asymmetrical at the base.

CONFIRMATION: The unique flowers and fruit—clusters of fragrant, usually six flowers or pea-sized hard seeds dangling on a thin stalk from the center of a ribbonlike, 3-to-5-inch-long bract.

### Common Apple
*Malus pumila* Mill.

Leaves alternate or in whorls, 2 to 3 inches long, grayish velvety beneath.

CONFIRMATION: The fruit—the familiar apple. However, these apples are small, sour and usually covered with pimples and riddled with worms. The trees, descendants of apple trees brought to North America from southeastern Europe and central Asia, have "gone wild."

# Leaf Simple, Margin Twice Serrate

**American Elm**
*Ulmus americana* L.
Leaves alternate, 4 to 6 inches long, 1 to 3 inches wide, more or less asymmetrical, dark green and usually smooth above. Secondary veins conspicuously parallel.
CONFIRMATION: The unique growth pattern of the mature tree, whose main branches rise like a column of water from a fountain, arching high into the sky with branchlets cascading downward. If the leaf surface feels rough to the touch (which occasionally is the case), it is rough only if rubbed in one direction, not both ways as with slippery elm.

**Speckled Alder**
*Alnus rugosa* (Du Roi) K. Spreng.
Leaves alternate, 2 to 4 inches long, broadly elliptical, tough and somewhat leathery.
CONFIRMATION: The shrublike character of this small tree, which grows only in the vicinity of water, lining the banks of streams and ponds. The ¾-inch-long woody cones remain on the twigs until the following season and are a unique characteristic, as is the triangular pith in the center of the twigs, which can be clearly seen in cross section.

**Slippery Elm**
*Ulmus rubra* Muhlenb.
Leaves alternate, 5 to 7 inches long, 2 to 3 inches wide.
CONFIRMATION: Although often indistinguishable in shape from the leaves of American elm, slippery-elm leaves can be recognized instantly by their coarse, sandpapery texture, which feels rough no matter which way you rub the leaf.

**Hawthorn**
*Crataegus* sp.
Leaves alternate, very variable, 1½ to 2½ inches long. According to authorities, there are some 800 different hawthorn species native to North America.
CONFIRMATION: The shrublike tree is heavily armed with vicious-looking thorns. It is the only tree of this kind that bears coarsely twice-serrate leaves.

**English Elm**
*Ulmus procera* Salisb.
Leaves indistinguishable from those of American elm (FAR LEFT).
CONFIRMATION: The growth pattern of this European import is distinctly different from that of American elm because the main branches, instead of arching upward, grow more or less at right angles to the trunk. This tree has been planted in many American cities, notably along New York's upper Fifth Avenue and on Boston Common.

**Hop Hornbeam**
*Ostrya virginiana* (Mill.) C. Koch
Leaves alternate, 2½ to 5 inches long, 1½ to 2 inches wide, closely resembling the leaves of sweet birch (p. 16).
CONFIRMATION: The typical fruit, a nutlet inside a papery sack, the sacks growing together in dangling clusters approximately 2 inches long.

**Gray Birch**
*Betula populifolia* Marsh.
Leaves alternate (occasionally, on shoots, opposite or whorled), 2 to 3 inches long, 1½ to 2½ inches wide, slightly sticky when young.
CONFIRMATION: Bark is dark brown on young trees, later gray-white. But unlike paper birch (*Betula papyrifera* Marsh.), the leaves of which are oval instead of triangular, the whitish bark of gray birch does not peel off in shreds, but adheres tightly to the trunk.

# Leaf Simple, Margin Lobed

**Sugar maple**

*Acer saccharum* Marsh.

Leaves opposite, somewhat variable, about 4 inches in diameter, palmately veined with three or five principal veins.

CONFIRMATION: Three or five lobes; the "angles" (*sinuses*) between the lobes are always rounded, forming the letter **U** rather than the letter **V.** Lobe margins usually entire.

**Red Maple**

*Acer rubrum* L.

Leaves opposite, about 3 inches in diameter, with three or five principal veins.

CONFIRMATION: The angle between the lobes forms a sharp **V** instead of a rounded **U**; the margins of the lobes are serrate instead of smooth. Leaf stems are red.

**Norway Maple**

*Acer platanoides* L.

Leaves opposite, very similar to those of sugar maple but usually somewhat broader, with seven instead of five main veins, darker and glossy on the underside instead of dull and light.

CONFIRMATION: The broken leaf stem exudes a milky sap; the two halves of the winged seed form an almost straight line instead of a **V** as do the seeds of the sugar maple.

**Silver Maple**

*Acer saccharinum* L.

Leaves opposite, 3 to 4 inches in diameter, five deep lobes sharply toothed.

CONFIRMATION: Leaves are green above, silvery below; the sides of the center lobe are not more or less parallel as in the previous maples, but diverge in the manner of the letter **V.**

**Japanese Maple**

*Acer palmatum* var. *amoenum*

Leaves seven-lobed and red-purple. This is not a native tree but an imported, ornamental shrub, included here only because of the beauty of its leaves. Together with the cut-leaf Japanese maple (p. 21), it shows how nature varies the same leaf design to almost any degree, from the full form of the Norway maple to the spidery shape of the cut-leaf Japanese maple.

**Eastern Sycamore or Buttonwood or American Plane Tree**
*Platanus occidentalis* L.
Leaves alternate, 4 to 10 inches in diameter.
CONFIRMATION: Conspicuous stipules at leaf base; base of leaf stem is hollow, fitting over next year's bud like an old-fashioned candlesnuffer—a unique feature among Northeastern trees.

**Tulip Tree or Tulip Poplar**
*Liriodendron Tulipifera* L.
Leaves alternate, 4 to 6 inches in diameter, extremely variable in size and form.
CONFIRMATION: The uniquely squared-off, "inverted" or saddle-shaped tip of the leaf, a feature not shared by any other North American tree; conspicuous large stipules encircling the twig.

**Sassafras**
*Sassafras albidum* (Nutt.) Nees
See page 14.

**White Mulberry**
*Morus alba* L.
See page 15.

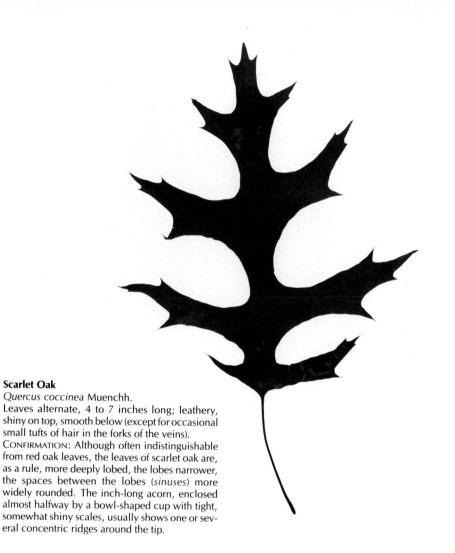

**Scarlet Oak**
*Quercus coccinea* Muenchh.
Leaves alternate, 4 to 7 inches long; leathery, shiny on top, smooth below (except for occasional small tufts of hair in the forks of the veins).
CONFIRMATION: Although often indistinguishable from red oak leaves, the leaves of scarlet oak are, as a rule, more deeply lobed, the lobes narrower, the spaces between the lobes (*sinuses*) more widely rounded. The inch-long acorn, enclosed almost halfway by a bowl-shaped cup with tight, somewhat shiny scales, usually shows one or several concentric ridges around the tip.

**Black Oak**
*Quercus velutina* Lam.
Leaves alternate, 5 to 7 inches long, 3 to 5 inches wide, leathery, shiny on top, extremely variable, with five or seven bristle-tipped lobes.
CONFIRMATION: Underside of leaves not smooth as with the otherwise very similar or identical leaves of red oak, but covered with a fine, dandruff-like fuzz or bloom that can easily be rubbed off between two fingers. Outer bark very dark, nearly black; inner bark bright orange or yellow. Acorn about ¾ inch long, one-third or more of the nut enclosed in a bowl-shaped cup covered with brown scales.

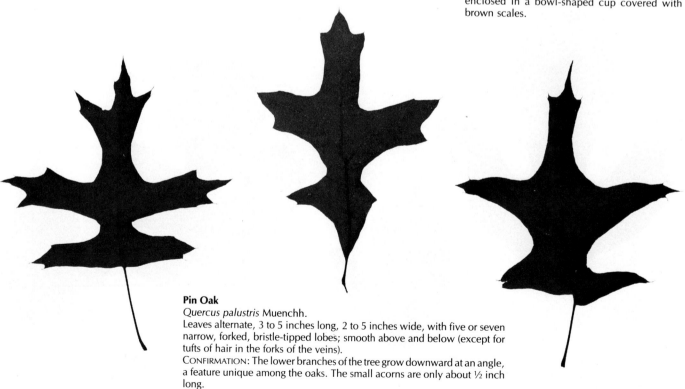

**Pin Oak**
*Quercus palustris* Muenchh.
Leaves alternate, 3 to 5 inches long, 2 to 5 inches wide, with five or seven narrow, forked, bristle-tipped lobes; smooth above and below (except for tufts of hair in the forks of the veins).
CONFIRMATION: The lower branches of the tree grow downward at an angle, a feature unique among the oaks. The small acorns are only about ½ inch long.

# Leaf Palmately Compound

**Red Oak**
*Quercus rubra* L.
Leaves alternate, 5 to 8 inches long, 3 to 5 inches wide; leathery, shiny on top, extremely variable with seven to 11 bristle-tipped, forked lobes.
CONFIRMATION: Underside of leaves smooth (except for occasional small tufts of hair in the forks of the veins), not covered with a fine fuzz like the leaves of black oak. The massive acorn is about 1 inch long and seems to sit almost on top of the very thick and shallow saucer-shaped cup.

**White Oak**
*Quercus alba* L.
Leaves alternate, 4 to 9 inches long, 2 to 4 inches wide, extremely variable in form and size; margins of lobes entire, tips smoothly rounded.
CONFIRMATION: Acorn about ¾ inch long, cup covered with hard, wartlike scales, enclosing about one-quarter of the nut. Bark light gray.

**Horse Chestnut**
*Aesculus Hippocastanum* L.
The leaves of this import from the Balkans are opposite and consist of seven (occasionally five) leaflets, 6 to 11 inches long, which are widest near the apex, tapering narrowly toward the base.
CONFIRMATION: The only other North American tree with which the horse chestnut could be confused is **buckeye** (*Aesculus octandra* Marsh. and *A. glabra* Willd.); but its opposite, palmately compound leaves usually have five leaflets instead of seven and are broadest near the middle, tapering toward both ends. And while the buds of buckeye are smooth and dull, those of horse chestnut are sticky and glistening, as if varnished.

**Cut-Leaf Japanese Maple**
*Acer palmatum* f. *dissectum*
Leaves consist of seven (sometimes six) leaflet-like lobes 1 to 3½ inches long. Like Japanese maple, this is not a native tree but an imported, ornamental shrub. See comments on page 18.

# Leaf Pinnately Compound

**Shagbark Hickory**
*Carya ovata* (Mill.) C. Koch
Leaves alternate, 8 to 14 inches long, with five (rarely seven or nine) leaflets.
CONFIRMATION: The bark of young trees is smooth, gray and finely striped, that of older trees broken up into narrow, shingle-like plates 1 to 4 feet long; their curving tips are often loose at both ends but always firmly attached to the trunk at the center. No other Northeastern tree has this kind of bark.

**Honey Locust**
*Gleditsia triacanthos* L.
Leaves alternate, pinnately and twice pinnately compound on the same tree (the latter only at the end of the branches), 6 to 10 inches long.
CONFIRMATION: The twice pinnately compound leaves, which are never found on black locust; the formidable, up to 4-inch-long, daggerlike thorns growing either singly or in clusters. Some cultivated varieties of honey locust, however, are thornless.

**Black Walnut**
*Juglans nigra* L.
Leaves alternate, 12 to 24 inches long, with 15 to 23 finely serrate leaflets.
CONFIRMATION: Leaves often have an even number of leaflets because the terminal one failed to develop. Split a twig and examine the pith: if it is finely chambered and buff-colored, it is black walnut. If the partitions are heavier and darker, and if *all* the leaves end in a terminal leaflet, the tree is **butternut** (*Juglans cinerea* L.); in that case, the leaves will be somewhat shorter, with only 11 to 17 leaflets.

**Red Ash**
*Fraxinus pennsylvanica* Marsh.
Leaves opposite, 10 to 12 inches long, with seven or nine finely serrate or entire, slender, pointed leaflets.
CONFIRMATION: A fine, reddish, velvety fuzz more or less covers the young twigs, the stalks and the underside of the leaflets. If this fuzz is absent, the tree is a variety of red ash called **green ash** [*Fraxinus pennsylvanica* var. *lanceolata* (Borkh.) Sarg.].

**Box Elder or Ash-Leaved Maple**
*Acer Negundo* L.
Leaves opposite, extremely variable, 7 to 12 inches long, usually with three, less often five, seven and occasionally nine leaflets, which also are very variable, ranging from simple to lobed and even compound.
CONFIRMATION: The characteristic double-winged maple seeds forming a sharp angle like little closing scissors. When you see these seeds on a tree with leaves reminding you of an ash, you have box elder, a member of the maple family.

**European Mountain Ash or Rowan Tree**
*Sorbus Aucuparia* L.
Leaves alternate, 5 to 6 inches long, with nine to 15 coarsely serrate leaflets on a more or less hairy principal stem.
CONFIRMATION: The massive clusters of orange-red, ¼-inch, berrylike fruit in fall and winter, much appreciated by birds. If the leaves are 6 to 8 inches long with 13 to 17 leaflets that are slimmer and more tapered to a point, the tree is **American mountain ash** (*Sorbus americana* Marsh.).

**White Ash**
*Fraxinus americana* L.
Leaves opposite, 8 to 12 inches long, with seven (occasionally five or nine) finely serrate or entire leaflets.
CONFIRMATION: Leaflets attached to the midrib by a stem; if stem is absent (leaflets sessile), the leaf belongs to a **black ash** (*Fraxinus nigra* Marsh.). If the twig has peculiar corky growths along its sides, making it appear square in cross section, and if it exudes a sap that turns blue upon exposure to air, it is **blue ash** (*Fraxinus quadrangulata* Michx.).

**Staghorn Sumac**

*Rhus typhina* L.

Leaves alternate, 16 to 24 inches long, with 11 to 31 sharply serrate leaflets.

CONFIRMATION: The lush, tropical, palmlike foliage and, in late summer and fall, the purple-red, conelike fruit clusters. Do not confuse with ailanthus (FAR RIGHT). If the leaflet margins are entire (smooth) and the leaves look somewhat like white ash (p. 23) except that they are alternate instead of opposite (and fire-engine red in fall), beware, because then the tree is **poison sumac** (*Rhus Vernix* L.). This tree, however, is only found in swampy grounds.

**Black Locust**

*Robinia Pseudoacacia* L.

Leaves alternate, 8 to 12 inches long, with seven to 19 small, thin, oval entire leaflets, surface smooth, blue-green above, lighter on the underside.

CONFIRMATION: Short, sharp, paired spines usually (but not always) cover the branches. Leaflets usually notched at the tip. Leaves never twice pinnately compound. If twice pinnately compound leaves occur at the tip of the branches, the tree is **honey locust** (p. 22).

**Ailanthus or Tree-of-Heaven**

*Ailanthus altissima* (Mill.) Swing.

Leaves alternate, 20 to 36 inches long, with 13 to 41 short-stalked or sessile leaflets.

CONFIRMATION: Leaf margins entire (smooth) except for one or a few large teeth near the base. But the best clue is the powerful odor of the crushed leaf, which smells like popcorn roasted with rancid butter.

# Leaf Twice Pinnately Compound

**Hercules'-Club or Devil's-Walking-Stick**
*Aralia spinosa* L.
Leaves clustered at the end of the extremely thick, spiny twigs. 3 to 4 feet long and 2½ feet wide, five to nine pinnae, each pinna carrying from six to 14 serrate or crenate leaflets, 2 to 2½ inches long and 1 inch wide.
CONFIRMATION: The enormous size of the leaves; leaf stems, branches, and trunk covered with slender thorns. *All* leaves are twice pinnately compound. If the leaves are somewhat smaller, only 1 to 3 feet long, the leaflet margins entire (smooth) and there are no thorns, it is **Kentucky coffee tree** [*Gymnocladus dioica* (L.) C. Koch].

**Honey Locust**
*Gleditsia triacanthos* L.
See page 22.

# Leaf Veins Parallel, or Nearly So

**Ginkgo**
*Ginkgo biloba* L.
Leaves clustered at the end of short twigs, 2 to 4 inches long, triangular or fan-shaped, leathery to the touch.
CONFIRMATION: This import from China, which nowadays is found in many American cities as a street tree, is completely unique, a leftover from the Age of Reptiles, instantly recognizable by its maidenhair-fernlike leaves with nearly parallel veins, wavy edges and often a wedge-shaped cut down the middle.

# Variations in Size and Shape

As mentioned before, the size and form of leaves can vary considerably within the same species, sometimes to such a degree that a leaf belonging to one species of tree appears to belong to another. As a matter of fact, variations among the leaves, especially those of certain willows and oaks, can be so great as to render impossible a positive identification from a picture alone. In such cases, only a physical examination of a freshly picked leaf that takes into account fine morphological characteristics (which may require the use of a loupe) can establish its identity.

In tree-identification books, leaf size is always indicated in inches or centimeters. When such dimensions are given—say, 4 to 5 inches long, 2 to 3 inches wide—they refer, of course, to more or less average leaves. Often, however, leaves are not average. They can be smaller, as on trees growing under marginal conditions and in spring, before leaves are fully grown; or they can be larger, as in the case of leaves collected from the lower branches of an old tree, from saplings or from vigorously growing shoots. Such leaves can be as much as two or three times longer and wider than the "average" leaf of the same kind of tree and are useless for identification.

Another potential pitfall is the fact that leaves growing on the lower branches of trees may differ markedly not only in size but also in form from those growing near the top. For example, while the lower leaves of black oak (*Quercus velutina* Lam.) are, as a rule, "typical," the top leaves (usu-ally inaccessible to the collector but found on the ground in fall and winter) may be indistinguishable in outline from those of red oak (*Quercus rubra* L.) and even from those of scarlet oak (*Quercus coccinea* Muenchh.). In the previous chapter, clues to the true identity of such look-alikes are given in the captions.

On the other hand, a high degree of leaf variability can sometimes be a bonus to the investigator. Sassafras and mulberry are typical examples. Both trees (pp. 32 and 33) bear three basically different forms of leaves, often on the same branch. This kind of leaf variation is a surefire clue to a tree's identity.

A good example of leaf variability within the same species is provided by the pictures on pages 34–35. All of these leaves are from the white oak (*Quercus alba* L.). I collected them from the ground in winter. They came from different trees of the same species and from both lower and higher branches. The differences in outline are astonishing, although the basic design is unmistakable.

Finally, on pages 36–37, in a series of seven photographs, I show how nature modifies a basic design (palmately veined leaves) from massive to delicate, demonstrating its adaptability to different environmental conditions, each variation original and new, each beautiful in its own particular way, each a testimony to nature's infinite resourcefulness, arousing my admiration and respect.

The giant tulip-tree leaf on the opposite page came from a three-year-old sapling. Measuring 13 inches in width, it is three times as wide as the average leaf shown for comparison at the right.

The 24 leaves belonging to the plant at the left, a common weed, are shown individually on the opposite page in a demonstration of the great variability of leaves in regard to form and size, even when coming from the same plant. The basic design, even if only in rudimentary form, is apparent in every leaf.

A sampling of leaves from several tulip trees (*Liriodendron Tulipifera* L.) ABOVE: A more-or-less typical leaf about twice natural size. OPPOSITE: A collection of leaves proving the high variability of the "typical" tulip-tree leaf design, the outstanding characteristic of which is the indented or inverted tip.

OPPOSITE: White-mulberry leaves. ABOVE: Sassafras leaves. BELOW: Ginkgo leaves. In each of the three examples, despite enormous variations of size and form, the character of the leaf design typical for each tree is preserved, making instant recognition possible to the trained eye. In the sassafras, it is the smoothly rounded margin, in the ginkgo the leathery feeling of the leaf in conjunction with the near parallelism of its veins, in white mulberry the crenate margins, together with the shiny leaf surface that make the tree glitter in the sun. OVERLEAF: A collection of white-oak leaves (*Quercus alba* L.) demonstrates the enormous variability of the leaves of this tree which nevertheless succeed in preserving a characteristic design.

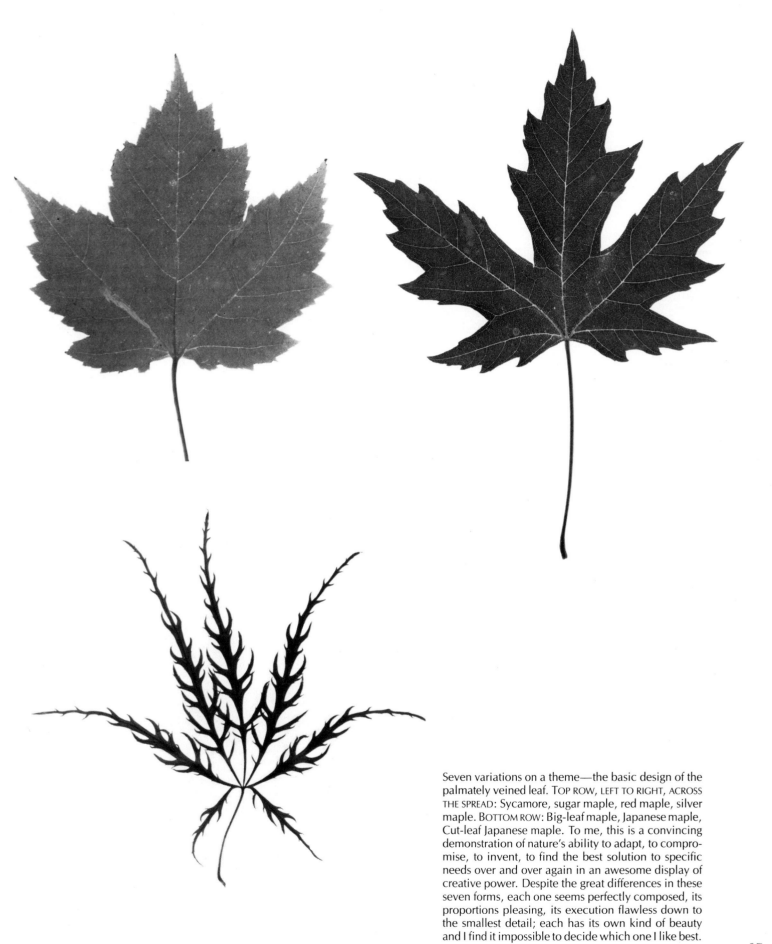

Seven variations on a theme—the basic design of the palmately veined leaf. TOP ROW, LEFT TO RIGHT, ACROSS THE SPREAD: Sycamore, sugar maple, red maple, silver maple. BOTTOM ROW: Big-leaf maple, Japanese maple, Cut-leaf Japanese maple. To me, this is a convincing demonstration of nature's ability to adapt, to compromise, to invent, to find the best solution to specific needs over and over again in an awesome display of creative power. Despite the great differences in these seven forms, each one seems perfectly composed, its proportions pleasing, its execution flawless down to the smallest detail; each has its own kind of beauty and I find it impossible to decide which one I like best.

# Leaf Structure and Venation

Leaves are factories; their purpose is to produce food for the plant to which they belong. This purpose—modified, as the case may be, in accordance with environmental conditions—shapes their design, which basically consists of two parts: the *blade,* which contains the chloroplasts—the organs within the cells that in turn contain the chlorophyll with the aid of which the plant converts water and carbon dioxide into sugar—and the *petiole* (stalk), which sometimes is absent (such leaves are said to be *sessile*).

The energy necessary to convert water and carbon dioxide into sugar is furnished by the sun in the form of light. Consequently, leaves are organized structurally and arranged on the plant to present as much surface as practicable to the sun. This surface is stiffened and kept taut by the *veins,* the other function of which is to serve as conduits for water and food.

The arrangement of the veins, the *venation,* provides a clue to which of the great subdivisions of flowering plants the owner of a leaf belongs:

In the *monocotyledons* the chief veins run parallel or nearly so, an arrangement called *parallel venation* (p. 44). This group of plants includes, among others, the palms, the lilies and irises, the grasses and corn.

In the *dicotyledons* the veins form a netlike pattern, an arrangement called *net venation* (pp. 40–43, 45–47). This group of plants includes, among many others, the maples, the oaks and elms, ragweed, thistles, sunflowers, petunias, geraniums and mums.

Net venation occurs in two forms. One is characterized by a single strong vein running the entire length of the leaf, from petiole to tip, from which lateral veins branch off like the barbs of a feather. Leaves possessing this type of venation are said to be *pinnately veined* (pp. 40, 43, 45); two typical representatives are the catalpa (p. 40) and the elm (p. 95). The other form of venation is characterized by several (usually three, five or seven) strong veins entering the leaf at its base from the petiole and spreading out like the fingers from the palm of a hand. Leaves having this type of venation are said to be *palmately veined;* typical representatives are the maples (pp. 36–37) and the sycamore (p. 62).

Leaves are attached to a plant in a manner that is constant for any given species. As far as deciduous trees are concerned, this manner of attachment can take one of three forms: *alternate, opposite* or *whorled.* These arrangements are illustrated on page 10 and provide a valuable clue to tree identification on the basis of leaves.

Leaves develop from buds, which may belong to one of two types. *Terminal* buds grow at the tip of a twig, while *lateral* (*auxiliary*) buds grow from the angle immediately above the point where the previous year's leaf was attached to the twig.

The opening of a leaf bud in spring is an event which, on a miniature scale, can provide a breathtakingly beautiful spectacle. Many times I have cut a twig bearing a few leaf buds, put it in a vase with water and watched the slow unfolding of the leaves. Four such sprouting leaves are shown on pages 48–51: dogwood, white ash, beech and tulip tree. To see these delicate young leaves unfurl their solar panels, to watch them grow and turn toward the light, can be a deeply moving experience.

Similar to an X-ray picture, the shadowgram of a tulip-tree leaf reveals the leaf's internal design. I made it by placing the leaf in an enlarger and projecting it, like a negative, directly onto sensitized paper.

A catalpa leaf, seen from its underside, is a typical pinnately veined leaf.

The leaf of a caladium, a houseplant, a typical representative of a
palmately veined leaf.

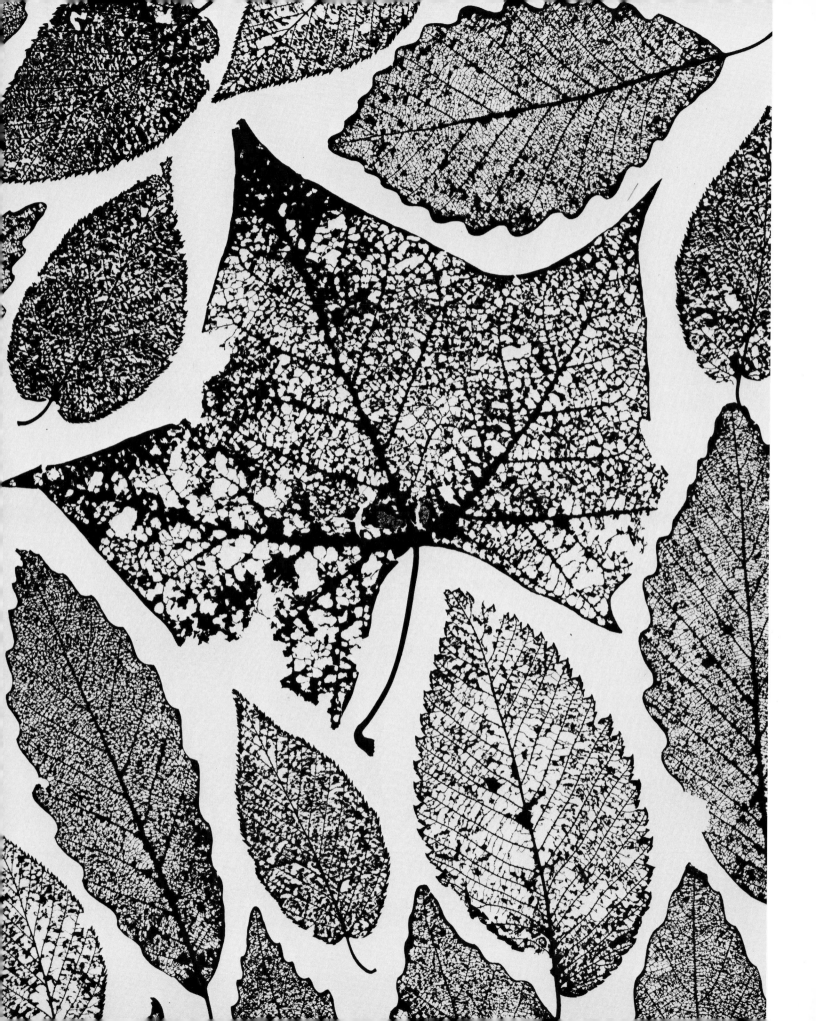

Some decaying leaves that I picked up from the ground reveal the arrangement of their veins. ABOVE: Chestnut oak. OPPOSITE: A sycamore leaf (center) surrounded by leaves of chestnut oak (wavy margin), slippery elm (lower right, twice serrate margin) and sweet birch (small, sharply pointed leaves with finely serrate margins).

ABOVE: Parallel venation in a grass leaf, a plant belonging to the monocotyledons, the group of flowering plants having only one seed leaf (including grasses, palms, bananas, orchids). OPPOSITE: Net venation. The picture shows the leaf of an unspecified plant belonging to the dicotyledons, the group of flowering plants having two seed leaves (including the maples and oaks, tomatoes, petunias and sunflowers).

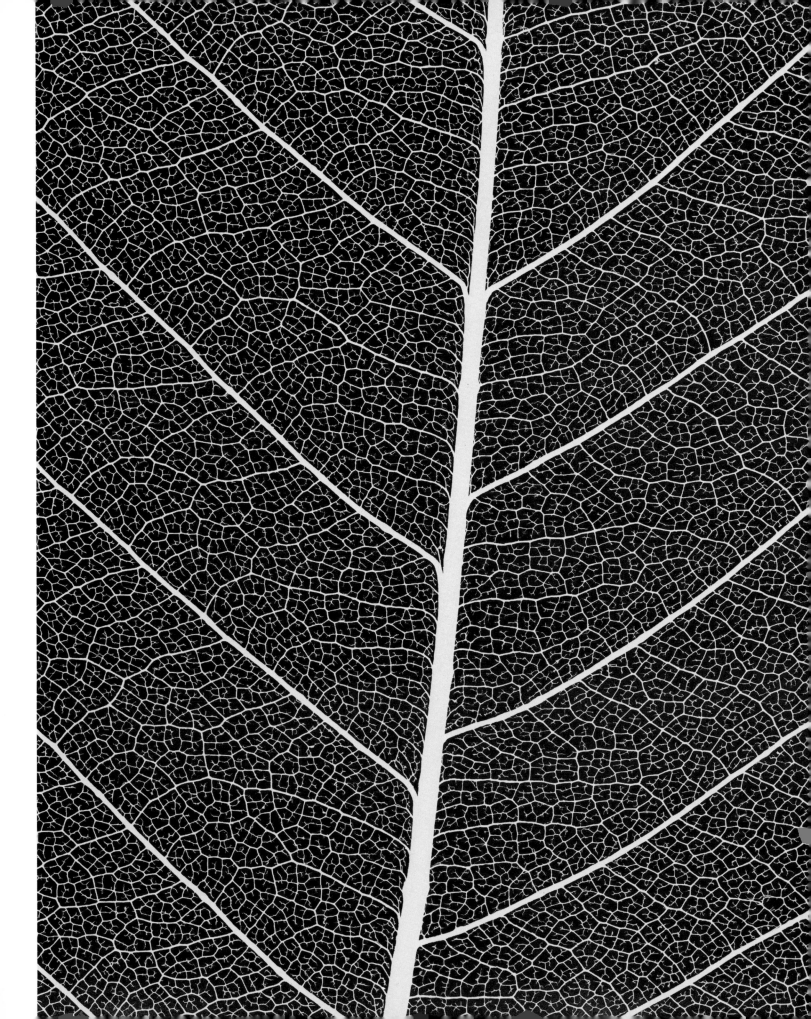

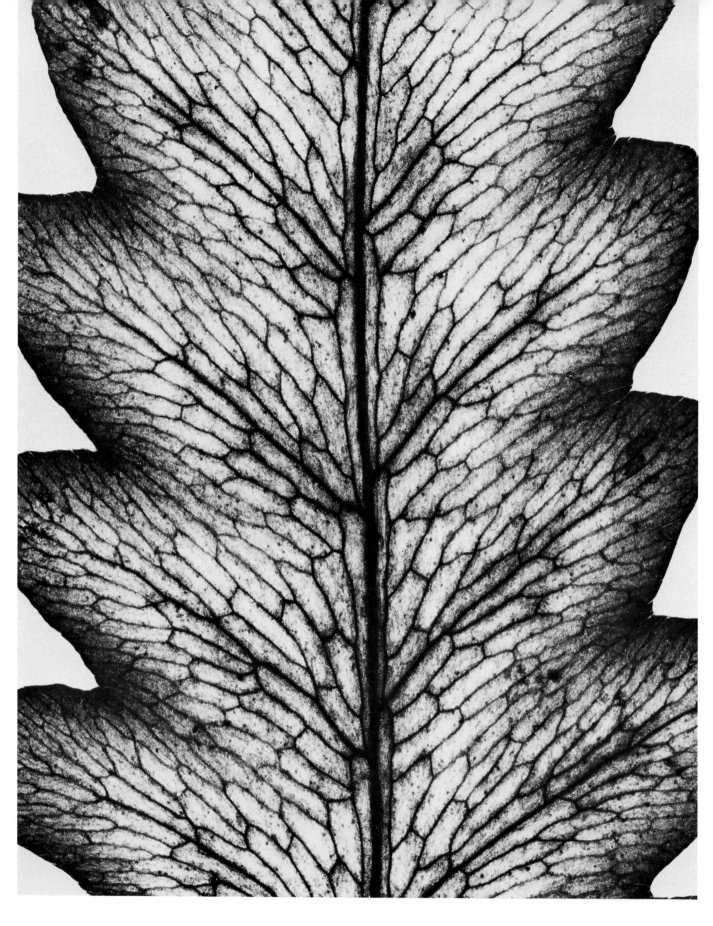

Venation in different kinds of leaves. ABOVE: An unspecified weed. OPPOSITE: Slippery elm. In both cases, magnification is approximately ten times natural size.

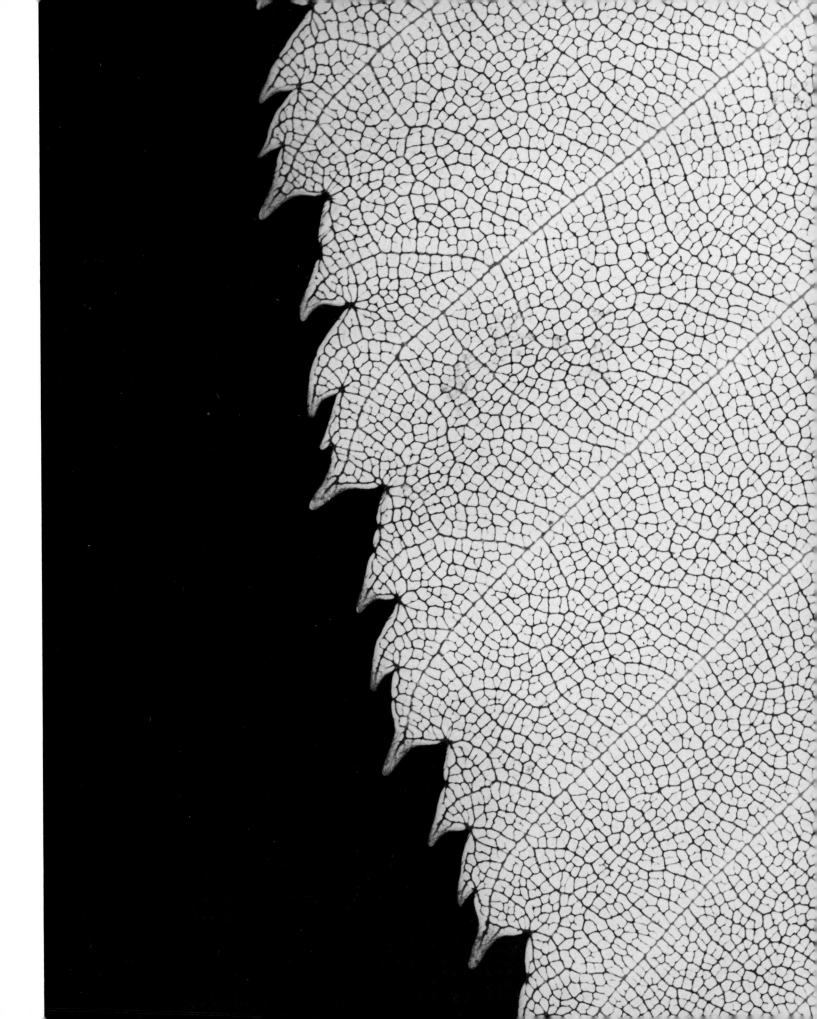

Leaf buds in the process of unfolding. ABOVE: Flowering dogwood. OPPOSITE: White ash. Magnification is approximately five times natural size. The way these leaves are folded and "packaged" in bud form is breathtakingly beautiful.

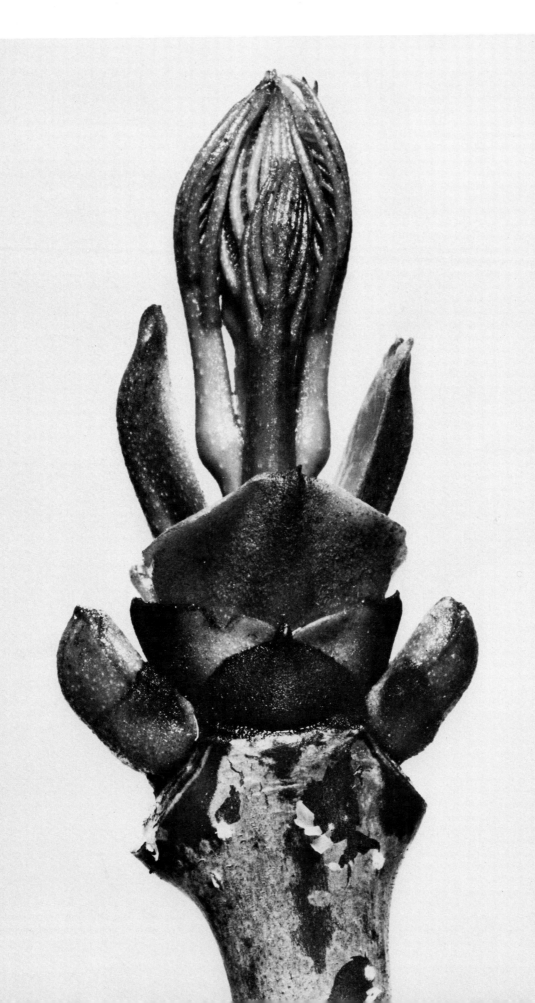

Leaf buds in the process of unfolding. ABOVE: American beech. OPPOSITE: Tulip tree. The slow but irrepressible emergence of leaves from their winter buds is a profound symbol of spring and hope.

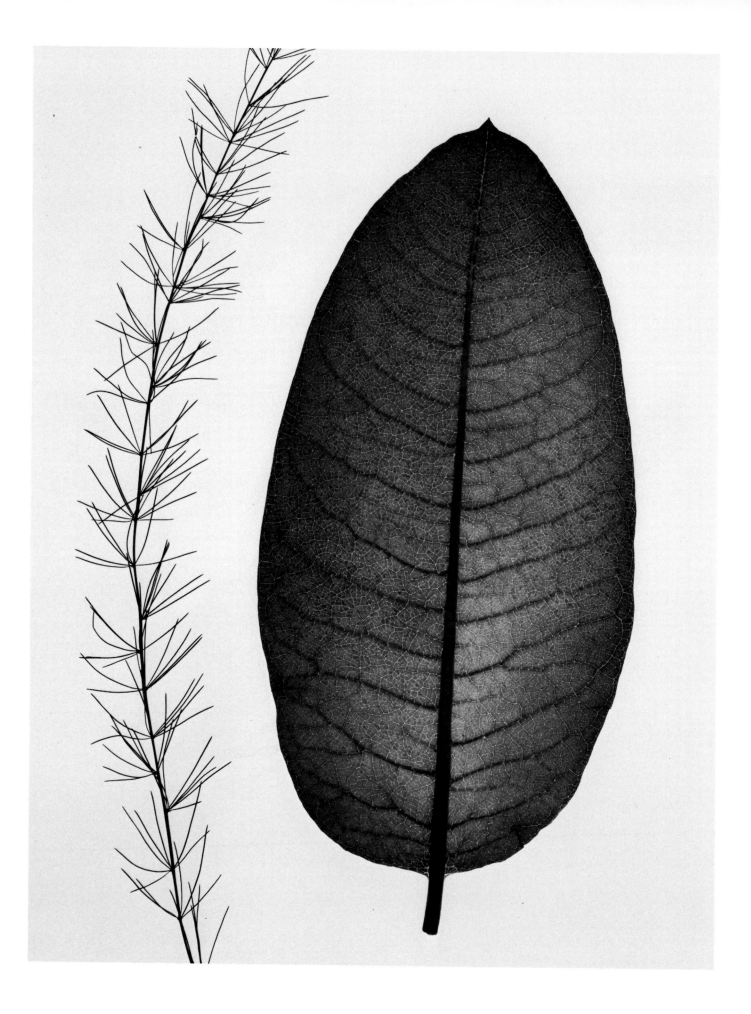

# The Variety of Leaves

Since no two leaves of even the same species are ever *exactly* alike, it is literally true that leaves occur in an almost infinite variety of sizes, colors and shapes. The largest leaves of any plant are allegedly those of the Amazonian bamboo palm *(Raphia toedigera),* whose leaf blades are said to attain a length of 65 feet, not including the 13-foot-long petiole. At the other extreme, the smallest leaves are the fronds of a duckweed *(Wolffia punctata* Griseb.) with a length of only $\frac{1}{40}$ of an inch.

But while extremes may be important for the record, as far as the interested layman is concerned, the true attraction of leaves is not size but shape. And in this respect we do not have to go to tropical forests or visit remote South Sea islands to find beautiful specimens because they grow right in our own gardens and yards, along our highways, in our forests and fields. Look, for example, at the picture on the opposite page. It shows the leaves of two plants that I picked within a short walk from my home: asparagus at the left, milkweed at the right. Both came from plants of about equal height—roughly three feet—yet what a difference in leaf size and design. The asparagus leaves are exquisitely delicate and wispy, the milkweed leaf is massive, coarse and thick. They represent extremes, yet each has evolved in accordance with the particular needs of the plant to which it belongs and the circumstances under which it grew. And between these extremes any imaginable configuration exists—and can probably be found by those with eyes to see within easy reach of their homes. The following 28 pages present a selection of such leaves.

It is relatively easy to see beauty in the unusual, the exotic, the bizarre; to see beauty in the familiar requires a special kind of vision—the ability to "see" with the eye of the mind. If you are one of the lucky ones who have this precious knack you will find marvels everywhere. Compare, for example, the leaves of sugar maple, sassafras, big-leaf maple, mulberry and tulip tree shown on the following six pages. See the similarities in these designs—and the differences. Marvel at the way in which nature has modified the same basic design in accordance with the particular requirements of different species of trees. Enjoy the various forms, each perfect in its own, almost "personal" way. What a source of inspiration for designers, artists—anybody with a feeling for elegant proportions, gifted with sensitivity to form.

Awareness of the intrinsic beauty of leaves can make any walk in nature a memorable experience. Leaves are everywhere and each, no matter how apparently humble and insignificant, has its own particular design. The smallest leaf of the most ordinary weed, seen with unbiased eyes, has some kind of beauty, manifested perhaps in a velvety surface, a finely toothed edge, an elegant curve or beautiful proportion between length and width. Do not forget the variety of outline, which can range from relatively simple but beautifully proportioned, more or less elliptical forms to the most complex and intricately curved designs, as found, for example, in the despised ragweed (p. 116). This is a field that anyone in search of a truly satisfying hobby, perhaps in conjunction with leaf collecting, drawing and photography, might want to explore. This kind of activity does not require investments in sporting goods, previous knowledge (because one learns as one explores) or trips to distant parts of the world, and it can be pursued year-round—in winter, by working with house plants (pp. 120–127). And it will reward the receptive mind with a deeper understanding of nature and her mysteries. It will lead to new insights and make the lucky person approach all of nature's creations with ever-deepening love and respect.

Sugar-maple leaf. The silhouette is unmistakable, unique.

Sassafras leaf. A trident among leaves, different and bold.

ABOVE: Sassafras in Connecticut. OPPOSITE: Big-leaf maple, California. So similar in concept, yet so different in execution; there is no end to the inventiveness, resourcefulness and imaginative creativity of nature.

OPPOSITE: White mulberry. ABOVE: Tulip tree. Studying the different forms of leaves, comparing them with each other, speculating about the "why"—what caused this leaf to adopt this form and another one that—can become a fascinating hobby—thought-provoking, mind-expanding, making us stand in awe before nature.

Opposite: Hercules'-club. Above: Sassafras. Pay attention to the arrangement of the leaves—the way they form a pattern, a "leaf mosaic" that permits each leaf or leaflet to receive the maximum amount of light.

Sycamore leaf.

Tulip-tree leaf.

OPPOSITE: Catalpa. ABOVE: Sweet gum. Each species of plant, each tree, each leaf, has its own character, grows in accordance with a specific plan, a design, a particular leaf arrangement such as the whorl of the catalpa or the five-pointed star of the sweet gum: an inexhaustible variety of pattern and form.

Ferns are representatives of one of the oldest groups of living land plants. OPPOSITE: The "fiddleheads" of the cinnamon fern (*Osmunda cinnamomea*). ABOVE: Maidenhair fern (*Adiantum pedatum*). The elegance and beauty of these plant forms defy description—they must be seen and experienced on a dew-fresh morning in the forest in spring.

Leaves of Venus's-flytrap (*Dionaea muscipula*), a carnivorous plant native to North and South Carolina. The tooth-studded leaves, hinged down the middle, bear sensitive hairs which, when touched by an insect lured to the plant by sweet-smelling secretions, trigger the "trap." The two lobes of the leaf quickly come together, their interlocking teeth form a cage, escape is cut off and the victim is slowly digested by the plant.

Two monocotyledons—leaves are parallel-veined. ABOVE: Papyrus (*Cyperus Papyrus*). OPPOSITE: Washington palm (*Washingtonia*), its trunk covered with a skirt of dead leaves.

ABOVE: Leaves of the coconut palm (*Cocos nucifera*), exquisitely formed like giant feathers, bringing to mind Venetian blinds by the way they modulate and soften the harsh southern sunlight to a particularly agreeable and soothing half-shade. OPPOSITE: The leaf-scar-studded trunk of an unspecified palm.

ABOVE: Prickly pear (*Opuntia*), a cactus native to the American Southwest. OPPOSITE: An unspecified agave. To protect themselves from leaf-eating animals, many plants have developed highly effective defenses. Some are poisonous (such as certain mushrooms), others sting (nettles) or cause blisters when touched (poison ivy, poison sumac), still others are studded with needle-pointed spines (most cacti, barberry, honey locust), viciously hooked thorns (wild rose and raspberry) or sawlike teeth (certain palms). And again, we can only admire nature's inventive creativity, this time in regard to defensive mechanisms.

Two kinds of aloe, their massive, fleshy leaves bursting forth with elemental power.

ABOVE: Coconut palm, its luxurious fronds arranged in the pattern of a feather duster. OPPOSITE: Traveler's tree (*Ravenala madagascariensis* Sonn.); the picture shows the basis of the giant leaves which may reach a length of 20 feet and resemble those of banana trees.

Dead leaves littering the pavement in fall—an opportunity to collect samples of leaves that grew near or at the top of trees, which normally are inaccessible to collectors. The left-hand picture

shows silver-maple leaves, the right-hand one a mixture of black oak, red oak, white oak and chestnut oak (see pp. 15 and 20–21 for more specific information).

# Leaf Arrangements (Leaf Mosaics)

At first, the picture on the opposite page may seem rather dull, nothing but a bunch of nondescript weeds growing at the edge of some woods. Upon closer inspection, however, an interesting fact will emerge: the leaves do not grow in random disorder (as one might expect), but in a precisely organized pattern designed to give each leaf the maximum amount of exposure to light. This kind of arrangement is called a *leaf mosaic*.

In this particular case, the leaves of the plant in the center of the picture (*Asclepias* spp.) are arranged in pairs of opposing leaves, each leaf pair rotated at an angle of 90 degrees relative to the pairs above and below it. This is by no means a unique arrangement, nor is it confined to herbaceous plants. Although not exactly common, we find the identical arrangement in certain species of trees, of which the maples, the ashes and flowering dogwood are the best-known representatives.

In other instances, leaves are arranged in a pattern according to which they alternate on opposite sides of the twig instead of facing each other (p. 10); representatives of this kind of arrangement are, among others, the oaks, birches and elms. Still other leaf arrangements exist in which the leaves spiral in various ways around a common stem.

What makes any kind of regular leaf arrangement (and irregular ones hardly exist) so thought-provoking is the fact that here we have case after case in which, instead of "undisciplined" or random growth, leaves are arranged with almost mathematical precision, as if in accordance with an intelligently conceived plan.

The ramifications of this discovery are mind-boggling. Imagine what this means. In the final analysis, plants, like all living things, consist of tissues made up of molecules which in turn consist of atoms. And atoms, science tells us, are "dead." In other words, plants consist of "dead" matter. How, then, is it possible that they grow as if directed by some intelligence in accordance with highly organized, functional patterns, instead of random ones, yet have neither a nervous system nor any kind of brain? In short, how is it possible that specimens of "dead" matter organize themselves in growth on the basis of highly sophisticated principles? Executing a plan that already existed in their genes, which are microscopic specks of matter? Something to think about . . .

The next 20 pages contain a selection of different types of leaf mosaics. In each case, the leaves grow according to a pattern that insures the maximum exposure to light for each individual leaf. For obvious reasons, the leaf mosaics shown here were carefully selected for clarity of organization. Out in nature, things are not always so obvious, and walking in the woods it may be difficult for you to disentangle the abundance of competing leaf mosaics. Yet the principle is always the same, apparent to the trained eye. Finding its manifestations in the flickering tangle of massed leaves seen against the sky is a worthwhile experience.

Two-year-old seedlings of tulip tree (ABOVE) and sassafras (OPPOSITE), photographed from above. The leaves grow in such a way that each receives the maximum amount of light thanks to a radial-symmetrical arrangement.

Two leaf mosaics. ABOVE: Shoots of slippery elm. OPPOSITE: Hercules'-club tree. Again, the leaves grow in the form of a mosaic that insures each leaf maximum exposure to light.

ABOVE: Dogwood. OPPOSITE: Wild grape. Dogwood grows in tiers, allowing light to penetrate between the layers of branches. The grapevine mosaic is organized in a single plane, avoiding any overlapping of leaves.

Leaf mosaic of Virginia creeper (*Parthenocissus quinquefolia;* OP-POSITE) and white mulberry (ABOVE).

Leaf-mosaic formation begins with the organization of the individual leaflets of a compound leaf. ABOVE: Virginia creeper, a palmately compound leaf. (Note that this particular leaf has six leaflets, an abnormality; the normal number is five.) OPPOSITE: Hercules'-club, a twice pinnately compound leaf. In both cases, the leaflets are arranged so as to avoid even the slightest degree of overlap that would deprive a shaded leaf of its full share of light.

Leaf mosaic of a weed.

Leaf mosaic of slippery elm.

OPPOSITE: Leaf mosaic of wild grape. RIGHT: Leaf mosaic of an unspecified thorny vine. In both cases the leaf arrangement is not only highly functional, but also forms aesthetically pleasing patterns.

ABOVE: Leaf mosaic of tulip tree. OPPOSITE: Leaf mosaic of white mulberry.

OPPOSITE: Leaf mosaic of slippery elm (see also p. 86, which showed a different form of leaf mosaic, typical of vigorously growing shoots of this tree). ABOVE: Leaf mosaic of dogwood. In both cases the leaves are arranged in such a way that smaller leaves fill the spaces left by the larger ones.

ABOVE: Leaf mosaic of sugar maple. OPPOSITE: Leaf mosaic of white oak. The decorative effect of such patterns is unmistakable and might inspire fabric designers.

# The Aesthetic Appeal of Leaves

Man's attitude toward nature can take many forms. The attitude of the scientist is different from that of the poet; the attitude of the strip miner differs from that of the ecologist. The bird-watcher experiences nature differently than the hunter; and so on. This chapter concerns itself with the attitude of the artist.

Seen with the eye of the artist, leaves are attractive in several respects. There is the beauty of elegantly curved shapes, often embellished with a "decorative" treatment of their edges in the form of wavy borders or various types of "teeth." There are colors in all the shades of the spectrum except blue. There is the special aspect of sophisticated compositions manifested in the form of leaf mosaics (pp. 83–103). There are textures ranging from shiny smoothness to bristling roughness. There are the netlike patterns of different forms of venation (pp. 120–127), often enhanced by color. In short, there is a fascinating world of form, texture, color and spatial relationships waiting for anyone with eyes to see, ready to stimulate and inspire the artistically receptive mind.

The pictures on the following pages show leaves and leaf mosaics that I found particularly attractive. The choice, of course, is a subjective one—not everybody may see what I saw in these leaves. In the field of leaf appreciation, feeling and intuition are all-important, descriptions are inadequate. Here, the pleasure is in the seeing.

An unspecified Connecticut fern surprises us with its aesthetically stunning design.

Staghorn sumac, that despised plant, is, in my opinion, a much-maligned little tree. One quality alone should make up for any drawback it may have: Where nothing else will grow, staghorn sumac flourishes. As a result, it provides much-needed greenery and even shade (it can grow to a height of 40 feet) on otherwise bare city lots. Besides, seen with unbiased eyes, it really is quite beautiful. Its leaves, which can reach a length of 24 inches, are exquisitely articulated in the manner of palm leaves—a stand of sumac can evoke an almost tropical feeling with its lush, feathery fronds which in fall turn a brilliant fire-engine red mixed with yellow.

On these and the following two pages I tried to convey something of what I see in sumac: a marvelously organized, stately shrub or tree of great intrinsic beauty, unappreciated only because it is too common—a "weed." OPPOSITE: A sapling. ABOVE: A typical leaf mosaic.

Staghorn sumac. ABOVE: Leaf mosaics as they appear in nature.
OPPOSITE: Close-up of one of the highly decorative leaves.

The almost heraldic beauty of two stately leaves, red oak (OPPOSITE) and sugar maple (ABOVE). Designers, look up and notice how perfect function (which we can take for granted as far as nature's creations are concerned) leads to perfect form. Let yourself be stimulated by such an experience but do not confuse inspiration with imitation. The principle is always the same; occasions for application are infinite.

ABOVE: A white mulberry leaf, fantastic, baroque . . . OPPOSITE:
A  marijuana leaf, classic in its severe formality . . .

A leaf of wild carrot or Queen-Anne's-lace, feminine, refined . . .

A leaf of wild grape, calling to mind a coat of arms, masculine . . .

The leaves of weeds, usually unnoticed, are often exquisitely formed. OPPOSITE: Ragweed leaves, arranged here in the same pattern in which they actually grow. ABOVE: Leaves from common yarrow or milfoil (*Achillea millefolium*).

ABOVE: The leaf mosaic of sugar maple consists of alternate pairs of opposite-growing leaves. OPPOSITE: The leaf mosaic of wild grape. Two highly decorative designs demonstrating the beauty of functional forms.

In winter, houseplants offer countless opportunities to continue seasonally interrupted leaf studies indoors. The variety of available material is enormous, the leaf displays spectacular. Shown opposite is a zebra plant (*Aphelandra squarrosa*) and, above, a red prayer plant (*Maranta leuconeura* E. Morr.).

OPPOSITE: Aluminum plant or watermelon pilea (*Pilea cadierei* Gagnep. & Guillaum.). ABOVE: Nerve plant (*Fittonia E. Verschaffeltii* var.).

ABOVE: A caladium plant. OPPOSITE: A houseplant.

Leaves of watermelon peperomia (*Peperomia argyreia* E. Morr.). The leaves, their designs creating the illusion of convex three-dimensional forms, are actually flat and even slightly concave.

# Index of Leaves